So Many Fives!

A STORY FOR YOU FROM
Big Math for Little Kids™

Herbert P. Ginsburg   **Robert Balfanz**   **Carole Greenes**

Illustrated by John Jones

DALE SEYMOUR PUBLICATIONS
Pearson Learning Group

National Science Foundation

This material is based on work supported by the National Science Foundation under Grant No. ESI-9730683. Any opinions, findings, conclusions, or recommendations expressed here are those of the authors and do not necessarily reflect the views of the National Science Foundation.

ISBN 0-7690-2872-1

Printed in the United States of America

1 2 3 4 5 6 7 8 9 10   05 04 03 02

Dale Seymour Publications
Pearson Learning Group

1-800-321-3106
www.pearsonlearning.com

Keisha said, "I am a very good mathematician. I know so many ways to show numbers. Do you want to see?"

Thomas said, "Not particularly."

"Sure you do," said Keisha.

"Here are my dolls," said Keisha. "How many are there?"

Thomas counted them. "One, two, three, four, five. There are five dolls."

Keisha said, "Very good, Thomas. There are five. Now I will show you five in so many different ways."

Thomas said, "Big deal."

Keisha said, "Just watch. Here's a drawing."

But Thomas said, "So? That just shows me your dolls. It doesn't tell me the number."

"Okay. I'll show you five," said Keisha as she made these dots.

But Thomas said, "Anybody can make dots."

Keisha said, "If you don't like dots, I'll show you tallies."

But Thomas said, "Big deal. Tallies! Show me something else."

Keisha said, "I can show five with my blocks. Here I separated the five blocks.

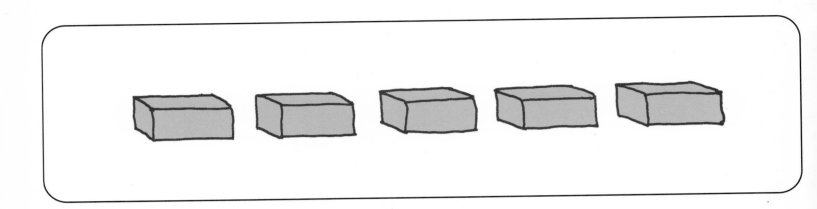

And here I put the blocks together. There are still five."

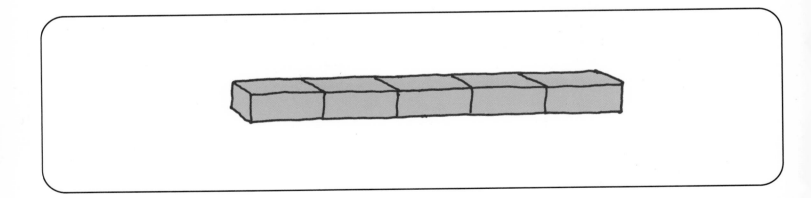

But Thomas said, "Blocks! Little kids play with blocks. Show me something else."

"Okay, I can say five," said Keisha.
Thomas did not look impressed.
"Listen," said Keisha. "Five. Five, five, five,
five! I'm saying five. Can't you hear me?"

"I can hear you," said Thomas. "But anybody
can say five."

"Look! I can write five with capital letters," said Keisha.

"But I can write five, too," said Thomas.

"I can write five in small letters," Keisha said.

But Thomas said, "I like capital letters better than small letters."

"I can make the Spanish word for five," said
Keisha. "Cinco."

"But I can make five in Spanish, too," said
Thomas.

"Wait till you see this one," said Keisha. "The Yoruba people in Africa have a special word for five. Arun."

"Not bad," said Thomas. "But is that the best you can do?"

Keisha was getting annoyed. She said, "What about Chinese? I can write the Chinese character for five. Isn't that amazing?"

Thomas said, "Actually, that's pretty good. But can you do any more?"

"Thomas, I showed you five in so many ways!" said Keisha. "I made a drawing. I made dots and tallies. I showed you five with my blocks. I said 'five.' I wrote FIVE and five. I made the Spanish word cinco. I made arun, the Yoruba word for five. I even wrote the Chinese character for five.

Look at all my fives! They are fantastic. I am a great mathematician! What else can I show you, Thomas?"

Thomas said, "Why don't you write it like this?"

"Oh, is that how you do it?" said Keisha.
"What a beautiful five!"